AFRICAN

GODS

ORACLE

AFRICAN

GODS

ORACLE

MAGIC AND SPELLS
OF THE ORISHAS

DIEGO DE OXÓSSI
ILLUSTRATED BY BRENO LOESER

ROCKPOOL

A Rockpool book
PO Box 252
Summer Hill
NSW 2130
Australia

rockpoolpublishing.com

Follow us! f 🅞 rockpoolpublishing
Tag your images with #rockpoolpublishing

ISBN: 9781922579485

Published in 2023 by Rockpool Publishing

Design and typesetting by Daniel Poole, Rockpool Publishing

Printed and bound in China
10 9 8 7 6 5 4 3 2 1

CONTENTS

INTRODUCTION

"Who looks outside, dreams; who looks inside, wakes up." **– Carl Jung**

I f you're reading these words, it's because you've made one of the most important decisions of your life: to look inside yourself, understand what makes you exactly the way you are and delve deep into the mysteries of your soul to unravel what prevents you from achieving happiness.

It needs a lot of courage to truly take this step, but I believe you have that courage, even if it's just lying dormant in some corner of your heart. I will guide you on a journey of self-knowledge based on the wisdom of the African gods and goddesses, and by the end you definitely won't be the same person who is reading these words now.

For those outside Latin America and its African-descended spiritual traditions it may sound weird, but worshipping the African gods and goddesses – called Orishas – means understanding that every element of nature is a deity in itself and that we can connect with these deities in order to receive their blessings and understand their wisdom and advice for our daily lives. The Orishas represent every power and natural element that exists in the universe, such as the air we breathe (ruled by Oshala), the fire that warms us (ruled by Shango), the sun that enlightens us and strengthens our bodies (ruled by Babaluaiye), the rivers and waterfalls that nurture life and resemble pregnancy (ruled by Oshun), and so on. With that in mind, every good thing that happens to us can be understood as a sacred celebration of life, and every bad situation can be seen as a spiritual imbalance that needs to be spiritually healed. In African spirituality, our gods and goddesses have the power of embodying their initiates and, through that, to mingle and dance with mortals – and we have the opportunity to see, touch and talk with them in a magical symbiosis that turns every ordinary moment into a magical moment.

I am Diego de Oxóssi, and for the last 20 years I've been practicing and studying African-based spirituality and its diasporic traditions such as Cuban Santeria, Haitian Vodou and Brazilian Candomblé; their historical and spiritual matters; and the ways this African-ancestry tradition became open and widespread to all black and non-black people in the Americas while keeping its ancestral power and identity, (re)creating African-based communities all over the world, and gathering people of all colors in the fight against racism and religious intolerance.

My first religious experiences began in early childhood, attending the Umbanda (a Brazilian spirits cult) temple where my grandmother and godmother were mediums. The white clothes, the smell of smoke and the chants enchanted me. Touched by a serious illness since birth and given up on by the doctors, my grandmother took me to a Babalosha or priest, who with the correct prayers, herbs and rituals, gave my life and destiny into the hands of the Orishas. In their mercy, they heard the call and at the age of nine the disease magically disappeared.

Years later, destiny became reality: in 2009, I was initiated into traditional Kimbanda (another type of Brazilian spirits cult), and in 2010, by the sovereign will of Oshossi (in Portuguese, Oxóssi, from whom I carry the name), I was initiated in the Orishas cult and became a religious priest, dedicating my life to spread their word across the world.

Since then I have led an Orisha Temple in Brazil in which we worship our ancestors and the African gods and goddesses, performing cowrie shell divinations and all kinds of magical rituals to help people all over the world achieve their goals and improve their lives through the work with the Odus – the "spiritual roads" that connect us with the deities.

From this life and my spiritual experiences, I've written five books that have been published in English worldwide, and with the Orishas' blessings, I now share some of this knowledge with you to use as tools to enhance your self-esteem and self-knowledge, awakening the best version of yourself.

What you are about to discover is an important lesson to follow your destiny and live in a harmonious way, even in the face of the most difficult challenges. The truth is that this is one of the greatest secrets of spirituality (and this is also true for material life): for our paths to unfold more easily, everything – absolutely everything – in the universe needs to be in balance: fire and water, work and leisure, positive and negative.

Sounds easy, but I've got lost in it myself a few times. I'm anxious by nature and, wishing to conquer everything at the same time, I forget that life is about balance and end up immersing myself in work 24 hours a day, barely breathing, as if the world would end if I didn't do everything I had to do at that exact moment! Until I finally understood: life has its time and good things comes naturally when we are not chasing them.

When I started allowing myself to live beyond my obligations, I almost didn't believe it: there's time to do everything that needs to be done and still enjoy life. The key to this turning point is learning how to turn dreams into achievable plans.

For this to be possible, however, I count on a little special help: the advice and guidance of the Orishas, who talk to us and influence our destiny through the Odus.

Technically, Odus are the signs of Orunmila/Ifa – the Orisha who rules all knowledge that exists, who knows all that has been and what is yet to come. Orunmila/Ifa is considered the Orisha of Wisdom, and is identified and interpreted during an oracle consultation with a Babalosha, or Babalawo. Odus connect Orun (African heaven) and Aiye (earth), and it's by these roads that the Orishas and all other energies travel and influence our lives. Just like everything else in the universe, the Odus carry within them the energy balance of good and evil, and their positive or negative aspects during a consultation will bring ire (good luck) or osogbo (bad luck) messages.

The Odus also represent the symbolic roads we take in life, with different opportunities and challenges according to our choices and free will. Each brings different possible destinies from which we can seek inspiration to face practical life, learn spiritual lessons to develop our inner selves and obtain advice about which offering or ritual must be done to ward off danger and attract good luck.

THERE ARE 16 MAJOR ODUS, AND THEIR NAMES AND MAXIMS ARE:

IRE Good luck	OSOGBO Bad luck
Okaran	
Those who have the Orishas' blessing are destined to enjoy happiness.	The dangers of the world are always lurking.
Ejioko	
The joy of life is seen through the eyes of innocence.	Those who deny reality will always live a distrustful life.
Ogunda or Eta-Ogunda	
Strategy is the path to success.	Stubbornness only brings unnecessary wars.
Irossun	
Knowledge is the greatest wealth one can have.	So afraid of what the future may be, you didn't act.
Oshe	
Brightness and glories to those who deserve them.	The shine of gold fascinates, but also dazzles.
Obara	
Happiness is the greatest wealth the gods can give us.	If you insist on your price, people will forget your value.

Odi

To persist when everyone else would give up is the road to success.

There is no easy way when pain comes from the heart.

Ejiogbe or Ejionile

Your reality is as big as you can dream.

The tongue is the whip of the body.

Ossa

Fire and passion run through your veins.

When the heart screams, reasoning goes silent.

Ofun

There are times to seed and there are times to flourish.

The future will never come while you're attached to the past.

Owarin

Good luck is only one step ahead.

When you always say "Yes" to others, you say "No" to yourself.

Ejilashebora

A cruel truth is better than the sweetest lie.

Lying to yourself is the most harmful spell.

Ojiologbon or Ejiologbon

Compassion is the path that leads to peaceful living.

When death calls, there's no place to hide.

Ika

"Impossible" is only a matter of opinion.	To avoid reality only makes you face the same issues again and again.

Obeogunda or Ogbe-Ogunda

Courage is the fuel that will take you where you wish to be.	Sometimes the best win is to choose what you're willing to lose.

Alafia

No harm can hurt those who live in peace with themselves.	A chaotic life is the result of chaotic choices.

Each Odu can bring messages from different Orishas who relate to these energies. In ancient Africa there were more than 701 Orishas, each of them having its own regional and/or familiar cult. Through the slavery of African people all over the Americas, they and their spiritual beliefs spread in what's known as the African diaspora, and these deities were gathered in 16 major Orisha families, or groups, worshipped all over the Americas, identified by the same Orisha's first name and subdivided into tens of "surnames", or "predicates". These surnames are only used in traditional rituals performed to initiates.

To use this oracle, you only need to know that the common names of these Orishas and their dominions are:

Eshu: God of movement and communication.

Ogun, Ogu or Ogoun: God of technology, progress, war and strategy.

Oshossi, Inle or Erinle: God of prosperity; the hunter who provides for His people

Ossain or Osanyin: God of medicine and the secrets of using leaves for health and magic.

Obaluaiye or Babaluaiye: God of health and disease.

Oshumare, Dan or Dangbala: God of long-lasting things and situations, of infinite and symbolic rebirth, and the nature cycles.

Nana: The Creation Mother; goddess of life and death.

Oshun: Goddess of beauty, love and pregnancy.

Ibeyi: The sacred twins, child god and goddess of creativity and innocence.

Obba: Goddess of independent women, the Brave Warrior; ruler of the wheel of life.

Iyewa: Goddess of vision and all things mysterious.

Yansan or Oya: Goddess of passion, work and progress; ruler of storms and the wind that changes things.

Logunede or Logun Ede: The teenage god of hunting, prosperity, happiness and beauty; son of Erinle and Oshun.

Aiyra or Shango Aiyra: The god of fire and thunder.

Shango or Aganju: The Royal Highness of all Orishas; god of justice and all pleasures of life.

Yemaya or Yemoja: The mother of all humans who feeds us with Her sacred breast to enhance life.

Olokun: Goddess of deep oceans and hidden secrets.

Aje Salunga: Goddess of financial wealth.

Oshoguian: The youngest god of Creation; lord of strategy and war that leads to peace.

Oshala, Oshalufan or Obatala: The father of all Creation; god of peace.

Oduduwa: The androgynous god/goddess who preceded world creation.

Orunmila/Ifa: God of wisdom and all knowledge.

In addition to bringing the messages of the Orishas about the events of daily life and how to solve the problems of our present and near future, the Odus also relate to our birth, determining key characteristics in our personalities and in the way we relate to people and the world around us. Just like everything else in the universe, they bring within them a whole universe of possibilities, positive and negative aspects, which you can meditate on.

What few people know is that far beyond the predictions of oracles, what really defines our lives is the way we understand the messages conveyed by them, the way they combine the lessons learned with our personal spiritual and emotional aspects and, above all, the way we put personal changes into practice, allowing us to become responsible for our own lives with the advice and guidance of the Orishas.

But if each of us is different from the next person, with different stories, desires, memories – and especially different personal energies and regencies – how can one set of fortunes, like those we see in the newspapers or on television, fit many people?

That's why such predictions can seem generic. When consulting an oracle, many people seek outward and miraculous answers so they don't have to recognize the greatest truth of all: that each of us is solely responsible for what happens to us – whether by how we react to a situation or by simply choosing not to act and not to question what happens around us, letting others and outside factors shape how life's circumstances will unfold.

The truth is that all honest and sincere transformation begins precisely when we use the insights of the oracle to start to question and reflect on who we are and who we want to become.

BEFORE WE BEGIN

Besides bringing messages from the gods, the Odus also define our personality archetype, the way we relate with the people and the universe around us, the way we deal with life challenges and how we walk through life to achieve our desires. Just like the signs of Western astrology, the Odus relate to our birth date, and before you start your journey into the magic of the Odus and Orishas, I'd like to thank you and gift you with the full interpretation of your Orishas Birth Chart, written by me especially for you.

You can use the *African Gods Oracle* by following the instructions given in How to use the cards, page 15. The Orishas Birth Chart is simply an extra tool which can enable you to assess the energies that rule your personality and its interpretations to meditate on how the Odu cards you choose when consulting this deck relate to your personal Odu, going deeper into the card meanings.

To get your Orishas Birth Chart, access the website www.diegodeoxossi.com.br/my-orishas-birth-chart, register using the promotional code african-gods-magic and I'll send you the link to access the full version of your Orishas Birth Chart, free of charge.

HOW TO USE THE CARDS

Traditionally, predictions and fortune-telling through the Odus are made with two different oracles, the Opele Ifa and the Merindilogun (also called cowrie shell divination), and represent the voice of the Orishas. Both methods can only be performed by priests and priestesses initiated in the Orisha religions and require years of study as well as several magic rituals that prepare the priests to understand and interpret the Odus' messages for those who come to consult. Through Opele Ifa and Merindilogun, it is possible to identify your Orisha spiritual regents, as well as which Orishas bless your life at this moment and which energies are interfering positively or negatively at this time, so that you can achieve your desires and goals. Consulting the cowrie shell divination reveals your desires, your dreams and goals, the prospects for your future, the ways to continue following a successful path or the reasons you have not yet arrived where you would like to be. Based on the interpretations of the Odus that are presented in these consultations, they offer ways of correcting problems and enhancing solutions for all kinds of issues of the body and soul including health, career and work, personal evolution and challenges, love and relationships, and more.

In this sense and out of respect for ancestral traditions, the *African Gods Oracle* is not intended as an oracle for forecasting the future. Rather, the deck you now have in your hands has been created so that the advice, lessons and archetypes of the Odus and the Orishas can be used as counseling and self-knowledge tools, turning your gaze within in order to help you reflect on anxieties and questions you may have, as well as decisions you should take (or avoid) to make the best choices and awaken your best version every new day.

The deck is made up of 36 cards. There is a card for each of the positive and negative aspects of the 16 main Odus we've already discussed. The other four cards represent the phases of the moon and its spiritual and symbolic influences over nature and our emotional aspects in life. On every positive Odu card you'll find a ritual that can be done at home to empower yourself and attract the Orishas' protection and blessings for your situation. Every negative Odu card has quotes and questions to meditate on to help you ask yourself how you've been living so far and how you can better understand the Odus' influence in your life.

Keep the four Moon Phase cards separate, and always draw one before choosing the consultation method.

This represents the lunar aspect that will guide the interpretation and advice of the other cards. The Moon Phase cards will guide you in the meditation process, indicating which subjective energies you must deeply engage with in order to search for your soul's answer and overcome any difficulties foreseen by the Odu.

There are three ways of consulting the cards to choose from: the Single Take with one card, serving as meditation and inspiration; the Triad with three cards, for reflections on objective questions of life; and the Cross with five cards, giving advice/interpretation for each area of life.

SINGLE TAKE: one-card reading

This is the simplest way to consult the *African Gods Oracle*. Shuffle the 32 Odu cards and, without thinking of any specific issue, draw a random card with the aim of obtaining advice and reflection for the present moment. I suggest using this method daily on waking as a motivational and meditative tool for the day ahead.

RITUAL OR MEDITATION

MOON PHASE

| PAST | PRESENT | FUTURE | MOON PHASE |

TRIAD: three-card reading

Thinking about a specific question, shuffle the 32 Odu cards then draw three of them in sequence and place them in a row from left to right. Notice whether each is positive or negative.

Card 1: What was favoring (a positive card) or preventing (if it is a negative card) the occurrence of the situation in the recent past?

Card 2: What favors or prevents the continuation of the situation's status quo at present?

Card 3: If no changes are made, what is the expected outcome of the issue in the near future? (If a positive card is drawn, then congratulations are in order; if a negative card, then pay attention: danger's on the way.)

Once you obtain your answers, you should reflect and meditate on how your actions and decisions might influence the situation in question – whether they might change or correct it, or simply maintain the status quo. One important thing to remember is that not making a decision – letting life take its course without you consciously acting – actually does mean making a decision, even if you're just deciding to leave it to fate.

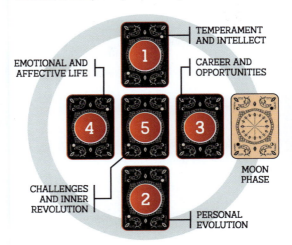

TEMPERAMENT AND INTELLECT

EMOTIONAL AND AFFECTIVE LIFE

CAREER AND OPPORTUNITIES

MOON PHASE

CHALLENGES AND INNER REVOLUTION

PERSONAL EVOLUTION

THE CROSS: five-card reading

This is inspired by the Orishas' birth chart reading, done through Orishas numerology (see Before we begin, page 13). Shuffle the 32 Odu cards and draw five in sequence, forming a cross (cards 1 to 4), with the fifth card in the centre. Each card represents an area of life:

Card 1: Temperament and intellect

This is the card that defines your innermost desires, values and ideals. It deals with the way you internalise and reflect on the issues of life and the universe, as well as the way you establish your goals.

Card 2: Personal evolution

Through this card you will understand how you walk the paths to your goals and how you struggle to achieve what you want. It is also the one that advises on the difficulties to be faced in the battles of life and the benefits you will receive at the end of each journey.

Card 3: Career and opportunities

This card deals with practical and objective reality, and material issues, governing your rational aspects and the ways in which you use your intellectual abilities and reasoning. It also gives guidance on the areas of study and professional activity that are favorable to you, and the paths of financial and career development.

Card 4: Emotional life and relationships

No-one can live without relating to others, and this is the card that will answer concerns about your emotions and the way you deal with others – whether in a loving, professional or family way. Through this card, it is also possible to understand what your ways of loving and being loved are, your sentimental paths and the most subjective aspects of your life.

Card 5: Challenges and inner revolution

This card represents the so-called "negative Odu", as it influences all the others, determining what is preventing you from achieving success in the areas you want, what personal challenges you will need to overcome and what lessons will be learned. It is also the card that gives the direction to carry out your inner rebirth, transforming difficulties into opportunities, canceling out karma and overcoming traumas and negative characteristics of your personality.

THE

OḌU

CARDS

1. OKARAN

Those who have the Orishas' blessing are destined to enjoy happiness

REGENT ORISHA: Eshu

KEYWORDS: Spiritual protection against all odds; victory and success ahead; good choices and decisions blessed by the Orishas

The positive aspect of Odu Okaran brings the strength and protection of the Orishas, stating that all choices and decisions made at this time will have their protection and blessings. More than that, it is through their blessings that the victories of your destiny are assured. Just remember to give thanks and honor what you have accomplished until now, practicing gratitude and creating a positive cycle of achievements from now on.

Eshu is the single regent of this Odu. Lord of contrasts, god of movement and communication, it is he who mediates our relationship with the other Orishas, and there is no path that can be accomplished without Eshu having acted beforehand to take our desires to heaven and bring the Orishas' graces back. Therefore, whatever your doubts or anxieties at the moment, calm your heart: what Eshu gives, only he can take away.

However, remember that even with divine protection, we are always subject to the weather of fate and therefore care and strategy are never too much. Just because the gods say "Yes", you can't take success for granted. After all, even if they lead the way and protect you from danger, it is you who will have to walk this journey, recognize the deviations ahead and avoid them as best you can.

Even so, it's time to celebrate! Fate smiles on you and it's time to reap the rewards of all the effort you've made to fulfill your wishes so far. Trust and move forward: happiness and success will come soon!

OKARAN'S EMPOWERING RITUAL

On a Waxing Moon Monday, right after waking up, mix a cup of cassava flour with 3 tablespoons of palm oil and throw it on the street in front of your home or workplace, asking for Eshu to protect you and open your paths to success.

The dangers of the world are always lurking

REGENT ORISHA: Eshu

KEYWORDS: Dangerous choices; spiritual weakness; victim of spells and harassment; evil energies and bad situations ahead

This is the most dangerous card of them all, as the negative influence of Odu Okaran brings dire foreshadowings which must be both feared and respected. No matter how hard you try to avoid them, we are all subject to the dangers of the world, the weather of destiny and, especially, the consequences of the choices and decisions we make every day. For this reason, the divine answer has already been given and it is time to withdraw and resign. To insist on saying "Yes" when the gods say "No" would be like awakening the force of a volcano and trying to control it with your hands.

Lord of contrasts, it is Eshu who commands the inevitable risks and catastrophes. Whenever he manifests himself in this aspect, Okaran shows his most terrible face and therefore demands caution, attention, care and precaution. Eshu, the Orisha owner of all paths and crossroads, alerts to all kinds of problems and dangers at this time of life. In order to calm the threats that pursue you, get back on track and make your days soft and light – exactly as life should be – you must urgently honor and please Eshu. Those who rely on the Orishas' protection, especially Eshu's, are less likely to have to face the world's blows.

Tricks and tragedies lie in wait. Still, despite the constant threats, the regency of Odu Okaran brings a great lesson: one cannot take a single step in life without taking risks. Learning the right time to act or hold back – to face and overcome life issues or to retreat and heal yourself with faith and courage – is the greatest mission for our evolution.

OKARAN'S SHADOW MEDITATION

Knowing that life risks are inevitable, am I consciously choosing which risks are worth taking in order to achieve my highest goals or am I simply struggling every day with battles I could have avoided by taking responsibility for my decisions?

3. EJIOKO

POSITIVE ASPECT

The joy of life is seen through the eyes of innocence

REGENT ORISHAS: Ogun and Ibeyi
KEYWORDS: Destined for success; generous; above-average intelligence; artistic and creative; avant-garde

Under the positive direction of Odu Ejioko, every moment must be celebrated as if there is no tomorrow. They say the eyes are the window to the soul and, at this moment, the glow of your eyes dazzles and your liveliness is contagious.

The time has come to take risks and rise to the forefront of life with the certainty that success is coming. To this end, exercise creativity and with childlike amusement and innocence discover how to overcome future adversities without losing kindness.

Orishas Ogun and Ibeyi gift you with intelligence and versatility, making you capable of discovering the best solutions to the challenges that lie ahead. To do so, you just need to perceive the countless options that the world has for those who face it with optimism and confidence.

Curiosity is the key. New opportunities will arise when you allow yourself to experiment and delight in what the journey has to offer. However, what is the use of starting so much and finishing so little? I know there is a fulfilling force within you that seems relentless and never-ending! And that's exactly why you need to learn to make the best of it, focusing your activities and efforts to complete what you start.

EJIOKO'S EMPOWERING RITUAL

On a Full Moon Tuesday, at the foot of a tree in your garden or in a park, light two candles – one blue and the other pink. Offer some candy and other treats, and a little soda to Orisha Ibeyi, praising the child gods and asking them to bring happiness and creativity to your life.

4. EJIOKO

Those who deny reality will always live a distrustful life

REGENT ORISHAS: Ogun and Babaluaiye
KEYWORDS: Temperamental; disobeys rules; stubborn and insistent; uncompromising; difficulty finishing what you start; naive

You'd like life to be a party, wouldn't you? So much excitement and willingness to face the unknown, however, needs to be balanced with a little rationality and maturity – two qualities you have to work hard to acquire.

Dreaming is good, but anxiety and naivety are your enemies right now. The real world is full of dangers that you won't be able to defeat, even wearing your fantasy-character armor. Willing to take the risk to discover and explore, you tend to deny reality and may end up getting involved in regrettable situations, only realizing your error when it's too late.

Remember: while tasting the flavors of life can be delicious, you need to learn to identify which ones really serve you and are good for you. Accustomed to constant experimentation, you have great difficulty in accepting the advice of those who have been where you are today, which ends up with you taking long tortuous paths out of sheer stubbornness. The fact is that this often hurts you and poses difficulties that could have been avoided if you put your pride aside and listened to the words of those who, out of love for you, just want to prevent you from repeating mistakes that have already been made.

EJIOKO'S SHADOW MEDITATION

Even though life is good and happiness is my journey's destination, how often do I confuse joy with a lack of seriousness, taking people and situations for granted while refusing to assume responsibility for what I say and do, as a child that never takes no for an answer?

5. OGUNDA

POSITIVE ASPECT

Strategy is the path to success

REGENT ORISHAS: Ogun, Eshu and Babaluaiye
KEYWORDS: Virility and fertility; strategic intelligence; pioneering; proactive and inquisitive; hardworking; communicative; adaptable

The positive regency of Odu Ogunda brings a period of inventiveness and practical achievements. Therefore the time has come to take the road to happiness and success, executing the ideas and plans that were waiting for a solution. For those who have Orisha Ogun at their side, there are no obstacles in the way.

Pioneering is the key word right now. Combined with the charisma and communication skills that Odu Ogunda lends you, you will stand out from the crowd for acting while everyone else is thinking. At the same time, it is also important to be inspired by the strategist capacity of this Odu. Have you ever heard the saying "no stitch without a knot"? Well, this is how your mind

should work to find the answers, and every step must have a reason and a purpose to avoid getting lost along the way.

Still, it is worth remembering that, as Ogunda is an Odu of battles, nothing will come easily to you right now. Therefore, fully dedicate yourself to the realization of what you propose: dividing your attention between more than one task will divide the quality and commitment to results – and between us, you're not willing to settle for less than perfect for yourself or others, are you?

At these times, you need to balance pride and efficiency: as satisfying as it would be to look at an achievement and think "I did it!", much has already been thought, planned and created so you don't need to reinvent the wheel for each new goal you want to achieve.

OGUNDA'S EMPOWERING RITUAL

On a Waxing Moon Tuesday, prepare two barbecued short ribs with no salt or spices. When ready, drizzle the first rib with 3 tablespoons of honey and the other with 3 tablespoons of palm oil, and put them on a pottery plate along with a can of beer. Light a dark blue candle beside the plate and ask Orisha Ogun for protection, intelligence and strategic thinking to achieve your goals. The next day, leave the offerings on a highroad (keeping the plate, which you can reuse).

6. OGUNDA

*Stubbornness only brings
unnecessary wars*

REGENT ORISHAS: Ogun, Eshu and Babaluaiye
KEYWORDS: Authoritarian; stubborn; tendency to lie;
difficulty in taking responsibility; jealous and possessive;
tendency to depression

The negative aspect of Odu Ogunda will constantly
challenge you and it is not for nothing that at every step
you will need to seek strength to continue the journey.
That, unfortunately, is the price to pay for deciding to
take a lonely path and insisting on doing things your
way, even if this "way" is the longest or the hardest.

With so much stubbornness – which you call
persistence – you need to be careful that the pioneering
power that bursts out of you does not turn into harmful
pride, which will lead nowhere. Resistant to admitting
you're lost, your natural reaction is to respond to everything
and everyone with arrogance and authoritarianism, which
needs to be controlled.

The warlike force of Odu Ogunda imposes on you the need to be right, but you've already passed the point of no return: I am sorry to say that you're the only one to believe that everything is fine. As Ogunda is the path of truth and righteousness, its reverse influence does not give you the talent to invent stories and be believed. On the contrary, from the first version of your story you change to others that don't support each other. By trying to deceive others you only deceive yourself. You will end up being discredited and when you're truly in pain even your closest friends will not help you.

For this reason, the answer and solution to your anguish lies in learning to ask for and accept help. Observe the examples of those who have already been where you are today and listen to the advice of those who care for you. It's better to be safe than sorry – otherwise, it won't do to repeat your tireless motto: "It wasn't me!"

OGUNDA'S SHADOW MEDITATION

While no-one grows up without struggling, do I have the courage to sincerely face myself and admit that I may be pursuing a lost cause, choosing to suffer instead of realizing that sometimes it's better to retreat?

7. IROSSUN

Knowledge is the greatest wealth one can have

REGENT ORISHAS: Yemaya, Ori and Oshossi

KEYWORDS: Analytical intelligence; great rationalizer; skill with words (especially writing); quick thinking; good adviser; eloquent and well-spoken; strategist

Thinking, reflecting, studying, meditating ... intelligence and the ability to rationalize situations to decide the best way forward are your greatest strengths. No wonder that, at this moment, your ideas and thoughts can transform the world around you.

Under the regency of Odu Irossun a word at the right time or the germ of an idea in an idle moment causes a revolution in your thoughts, ultimately resulting in an ambitious project that allows you to change everything around you and your dear ones.

At the same time, your ability with words makes you a good adviser and speaker, but you must be careful not to get lost in theories and end up being misunderstood.

Consciously choose your words and gestures so that what you want to convey can be comprehended by anyone.

Initiative and achievement are the key words that govern your paths and your personal evolution. This should be your motto today and always; after all, faith and awareness of yourself – your qualities and your limitations – make you a great thinker. Your decisions at this time should be based on rationality and stability.

IROSSUN'S EMPOWERING RITUAL

On a Waxing Moon Saturday, using a pencil, write all your best wishes on a piece of white paper in honor of Ori – your spiritual head Orisha. Make a hole on the top of a melon and put the paper inside, drizzling it with honey and olive oil. Light a seven-day white candle and fix it in the hole, then put the melon with its candle in a safe place above head height until the candle is burnt. On the next day, dispatch the melon into the sea or a river.

8. IROSSUN

NEGATIVE ASPECT

So afraid of what the future may be, you didn't act

REGENT ORISHAS: Oya, Nanna and Iku (the Death)
KEYWORDS: Genius and authoritative; aggressive when speaking; stands alone in the crowd; relationship issues with mother; tendency to take responsibility for the problems of others; thinks a lot but acts little, leading to stagnation; serious illnesses with a spiritual background

Grief and resentment mark this moment in life, and the negative influence of Odu Irossun reinforces the difficulties in forgetting and overcoming the wounds and scars of the past. With that, the smallest spark can cause an explosion of authoritarianism and violence, especially when situations get out of control and things don't happen as you determined. In these moments, you have the feeling that the world has decided to provoke you – and you won't allow your ability to be tested or questioned by anyone.

You carry the certainty that you are always right; after all, with so much thinking and reflecting on all the possibilities, it's impossible that you haven't found the absolute truth, isn't it? No, it's not! The challenge is to understand that there are no absolutes, and that communication is the key to recognizing your full potential. The truths of life are relative – as are the paths of everyone around you.

This excess of self-confidence causes you to take on roles that should not concern you: you end up carrying the weight of the world on your shoulders, which pulls you away from the people who care for you, even when your sincere desire is to care for and protect those in need. If you allow things to continue this way you will inevitably end up alone and abandoned, even in a crowd, as if despite all your efforts you seem invisible and insensitive to others.

Learning to forgive those who have hurt you and, above all, learning to truly forgive yourself will transform your life and your ways.

The time has come to let go of the guilt and burden of past mistakes, and the key to overcoming these hurts is forgiveness. Learning to forgive those who have hurt you and, above all, to forgive yourself sincerely and truly, will transform your life and your ways.

IROSSUN'S SHADOW MEDITATION

It seems that people around me are always making me responsible for them and their obligations, as if I was in charge of their lives. How many times have I put myself in roles that are not mine, assuming positions where I'd rather they did things my way instead of letting them do things their way (which I believe to be wrong)?

9. OSHE

POSITIVE ASPECT

Brightness and glories to those who deserve them

REGENT ORISHA: Oshun

KEYWORDS: Charming and elegant; likely to achieve fame; good taste and refinement; good at generating wealth; loving and sentimental; ingenious; knows how to create plans and execute them; proactive

The shine and fascination of gold defines your moment in life and you will attract glances and recognition wherever you go, walking through life as if you were on a catwalk. However, you must take care that such recognition and power do not go to your head and make you confuse ambition and greed. While the first boosts you, making you always seek the best that the world has to offer, the second awakens the worst facets of your personality – and it's no use shining if there's no audience to applaud you.

Your good taste and charisma, combined with the positive financial moment that shines on your path, allow you to experience the pleasures of life and recognize that if there is time to fulfill obligations there is also time for enjoyment and relaxation. The key to victory and prosperity in all aspects is learning to use your intuition and your personal magic. These are the divine powers that the Orishas have put into your life, and by learning to tap into them you will discover that unlimited happiness and abundance are at your disposal.

Oshe is also the Odu of love and relationships, of motherhood and fertility. However, to experience these blessings, you must first sincerely understand that love is based on confidence and partnership – not on demand and dependence. When you truly love yourself, rest assured: the universe will repay you and people will love you for who you are, not what you have.

OSHE'S EMPOWERING RITUAL

On a Full Moon Saturday, prepare a herbal bath by boiling sunflower seeds, cloves, cinnamon, star anise, nutmeg and a whole sunflower bud (or substitute another large, non-toxic, bright red or yellow flower if necessary). Let it cool, then strain and add a gallon (4 liters) of clear water and 21 short sprays of your favorite perfume. Using the sunflower bud as a bath sponge, soap up from head to toe then rinse off with the herbal bath.

10. OSHE

The shine of gold fascinates, but also dazzles

REGENT ORISHAS: Iya Mi Agba (the Eldest Mothers)
KEYWORDS: Malicious; tendency to lie, pretend and dissimulate; emotionally dependent; greedy; jealous and vindictive; lives in dispute; spiteful, difficult to forgive

How much heartache and unrequited love! Under the influence of Odu Oshe in its negative aspect, it seems almost impossible to find someone who returns all the love you have to give. But is it really better to be in bad company than to be alone? Harder than allowing yourself to be loved is learning to love yourself; facing up to your worst faults so you are able to correct them. Therein lies one of the biggest challenges for your personal revolution: to look inside and recognize yourself, empowering your skills but working on your issues to reach the best version you can be.

You've been accustomed to pointing fingers at others as if you have no part in what happens to you, forgetting that the key to personal growth is taking responsibility for your choices and paths. You are also able to invent stories and situations that almost achieve what you want ... But who's really believing them?

The golden shine of Odu Oshe will naturally attract eyes wherever you go, but its negative aspect makes you a sponge for negative energies. No wonder that even when you have someone there is still an open wound in your heart. Loneliness frightens you as the night frightens a child – and that's the way you've been treating your relationships. Need and jealousy hardly combine with happiness and are an open door to depression and negative feelings, which will inhabit your thoughts at the most painful moments. How about taking a deep breath and recognizing that you're human too?

OSHE'S SHADOW MEDITATION

Love, fame and glory might seem a nice place to be, but do I allow myself to be vulnerable? Am I showing myself the way I truly am or am I living like a fantasy character just to feel liked and approved by people around me?

11. OBARA

POSITIVE ASPECT

Happiness is the greatest wealth the gods can give us

REGENT ORISHAS: Oshossi, Logunede and Shango

KEYWORDS: Natural beauty; charisma; humorous; makes friends easily; skill with sales and money; great at selling yourself and your ideas

Prosperity and good luck mark this moment in your life under the positive direction of Odu Obara. You were born to be happy, to share joy and good humor. Your open smile lights up the place and enchants everyone around you – no wonder this is the ideal time to make new friends and establish personal or commercial partnerships.

It's also a good time to search for the best opportunities in everything that happens to you personally, but especially in material and financial matters. A salesperson by nature, the ease with which your ideas, projects and products are accepted is the key to your success at this stage. How about starting to take them off the page and transform the reality around you into new ways to make money?

With so much excitement within you, it is necessary to control your feelings a little, because sometimes your joy can be confused with a lack of seriousness. Therefore, it is important to know how to gauge the measure of dreams and reality that you show to the world around you in order to enchant without seeming childish or inconsequential.

Still, under the protection of the Orishas Oshossi, Logunede and Shango, you have many reasons to celebrate, as Odu Obara guarantees you bliss whatever your purpose. Its motto is "If there is no easy way, there is also no impossible way". Keep your confidence and smile in the certainty that the paths ahead will lead to the great victories that the Orishas are preparing for you.

OBARA'S EMPOWERING RITUAL

On the last night of Waxing Moon, prepare a Power Pot in a glass jar with all the kinds of seeds and grains you have in your kitchen pantry, adding one at a time in layers. Between these layers, put six coins, a few drops of your favorite perfume, and your wealth and prosperity wishes written on a piece of white paper. On top of the last layer place a seashell and a candy and put the Power Pot in the highest place in your home or work. After six days, bury the contents (except the glass jar, which can be reused) of your Power Pot in your garden or in a pot plant.

12. OBARA

If you insist on your price, people will forget your value

REGENT ORISHAS: Oshossi, Logunede and Shango
KEYWORDS: Lacks initiative; uncompromising; proud; talks too much and doesn't listen to people; naive, trusts too much; tendency to lie and fantasize; tendency to depression, especially due to childhood trauma

The influence of Odu Obara in its negative aspect brings out the most puerile nuances of your personality, reinforcing your stubbornness, naivety and – sometimes – tyranny when your wishes are not met. All of this, in fact, can be defined in a single word: anxiety. By denying your feelings, you delude yourself into expecting the people around you to keep up. When they're not able to understand your feelings and actions, you get frustrated and flirt with paranoia and depression.

As a child in the body of an adult, you tend to hold others accountable for your actions and always expect someone to come to the rescue and solve the problems around you – especially those you caused yourself. Life is good and should be lived well, but it is necessary to accept that sometimes the demands of adult life will overcome your dreams and desires, and it's time to pay attention to those demands so you can get back on track.

As an Odu linked to wealth and abundance of resources, its negative influence indicates lack of control over your finances, often bordering on uncontrollable consumerism. Like any energy source, prosperity can go through times of ebb and flow, and if you don't prepare you'll end up repeatedly mired in bureaucratic problems, legal disputes and debts.

You can and should dream bigger and bigger, but you must also accept reality and understand that each thing has its time – and usually that's not going to come as fast as you want. Here's the biggest challenge for your inner revolution: to put aside the fantasy and take, once and for all, responsibility for your actions and decisions – including when you decide not to make any! For everything in life there is a price to be paid, the reward for taking your life into your own hands is full freedom, and the pleasure of being truly free is far greater than the setbacks fate may bring.

OBARA'S SHADOW MEDITATION

Considering all life's goals and relationships I'm living now, do I understand the difference between the cost and the value of all the things I do, have and pursue? And based on the way I present myself to the world, do I offer my price or my value to others?

13. ODI

To persist when everyone else would give up is the road to success

REGENT ORISHAS: Eshu, Ogun and Babaluaiye
KEYWORDS: Analytical intelligence; persistent; good memory; hard worker; careful and zealous about what and who you like; seeking excellence and perfection

You've been facing challenges for as long as you can remember and it seems as if those obstacles will never end. Unfortunately, the reality is more or less like that. Despite this, however, you can already consider yourself a winner: no-one else in the world has your stamina and willpower. "Persisting when anyone else would give up" is your motto and the secret to your success – and I guarantee it will come! Wasn't it you yourself who set out to be more and better; to excel in everything you do and each day become more complete and independent?

The real world and adult life have their difficulties and always will, but it is useless to surrender believing that the giants ahead are stronger. On the contrary: you've got used to fighting for what you want and now is not the time to give it all up. Remember how many bigger and more difficult challenges have been overcome and find your inner strength. You are smart and capable, and no challenge is bigger than your ability to overcome it. Believe in this and the reality around you will certainly change.

The universe gives back what we project to it and most of the setbacks of the current moment are nothing more than reflections of your thoughts. To avoid this, it is necessary to resist the weather of destiny and the harsh criticisms you make of yourself and the people around you, and rediscover your value. By loving yourself first, you will surely communicate that love to the world around you and be recognized by it.

ODI'S EMPOWERING RITUAL

On a Waning Moon Monday, prepare a herbal bath by boiling leaves from mango and orange trees with rosemary. Let it cool and add a gallon (4 liters) of clear water. After your regular bath, rinse with the herbal bath from the neck down, asking Eshu for spiritual cleansing and protection against all evil. You can also use this herbal bath for cleansing your house's or office's energies: for that, wipe a cloth dampened with bath water on the floor, and on the door and window frames.

14. ODI

There is no easy way when pain comes from the heart

REGENT ORISHAS: Eshu, Ogun and Babaluaiye

KEYWORDS: Does not tolerate weakness and incompetence; gossips; difficulty keeping secrets; marital infidelity; superstitious; doubts everything and everyone; unyielding; jealous; lonely, prefers to live isolated from others

Resignation is the motto for this moment in your life. The negative influence of Odu Odi brings a path of struggles and difficulties that often seem insurmountable. As much as you have confidence in yourself, the universe puts you to the test and it feels like each obstacle comes faster and is harder than the previous one, testing your patience to the point where you stop believing in the future.

However, as you are willing to seek perfection you must be prepared to face all demons – yours and others – as if they were light summer breezes. With the right amount of intelligence and effort combined with the strength and protection of the Orishas, no challenge will be greater than your ability to overcome it – and to win is your life mission! But be aware that all this steely force does not turn into stubbornness and inflexibility. If you allow these traits to emerge in your personality, they will inevitably cause you to snatch defeat from the jaws of victory, making you even lonelier than you already are (even in a crowd).

The biggest lesson for your inner revolution is to learn to keep your successes and plans secret. Odu Odi itself is a delicate energy, especially in its negative aspect. So to avoid fate's setbacks, learn to keep quiet about yourself and others. Remember: what is neither said nor known cannot be envied or destroyed.

ODI'S SHADOW MEDITATION

Is the level of excellence I demand from myself and others around me truly achievable or am I demanding the impossible? If I'm never satisfied with the results I get, will I keep manifesting my dissatisfaction in a never-ending self-sabotage cycle?

15 EJIOGBE

Your reality is as big as you can dream

REGENT ORISHAS: Oshoguian (the youngest Oshala) and Shango Aiyra

KEYWORDS: Social and political ability; eloquent and convincing; able to multitask; searches for excellence; ambitious; curious; freedom lover

Horizons of grandeur and achievement are what guide your steps right now. However, there is always the feeling that someone is chasing you, ready to betray your trust and pull the rug out from under you at any moment. Calm down and take a deep breath. The world is indeed a dangerous place for the unsuspecting, but you don't need to be alert all the time – after all, the earth revolves around the sun and not around you.

Look inside yourself and realize you are capable, deserving and victorious – that's why you are already reaping the great fruits of destiny, even when all circumstances say otherwise. Still, even when the path

ahead is positive and promising, a shadow hangs over your soul. To defuse these conflicts, you need to be the first to believe in yourself, sincerely and honestly. Only then will the people around you also truly recognize your worth and no longer agree simply to avoid angering you so you won't fall on them with fury.

Your discretion and air of authority allow you to be accepted in the most diverse groups, and even serve as a mediator in conflicts. However, this social fluency is marked by many betrayals and persecutions. If you decide to go through life according to your own will, you must be careful not to cross the boundary between ambition and greed, as your tendency to reshape truth and reality can cause you to stumble – and once you've left everyone behind, there won't be anyone to catch you if you fall.

EJIOGBE'S EMPOWERING RITUAL

On a New Moon Friday and then for the next seven days, before going to sleep take a head-to-toe bath of clear water mixed with a pinch of indigo powder (or African waji if you can find it where you live) and a few drops of your favorite perfume, asking Oshoguian to give you balance in life and clear thoughts so you can face life's challenges. After the bath, wear white or very light clothes.

16. EJIONILE

The tongue is the whip of the body

REGENT ORISHAS: Oshoguian (the youngest Oshala) and Shango Aiyra

KEYWORDS: Gets sick of things easily; flexible ethics and morals; has violent passions; impulsive and vindictive; tendency to pretend and lie; enjoys intrigue; lives surrounded by confusion and falsehood

Under the regency of Odu Ejionile, you're already tired of so much confusion and persecution. But, honestly, how many of them have you not brought upon yourself? As much as you make a conscious effort to remain aloof from the intrigues and lies of the world around you, there is an inner force that discreetly pushes you towards them, making it seem as if you flee from confusion but confusion runs after you (or is it the other way around?).

If in its positive aspect the Odu Ejiogbe guarantees great conquests and victories, in its negative aspect (called Ejionile) it becomes fate's cruelest boss. In this way, the subtle difference between ambition and greed, or telling a lie and hiding the truth, must be learned urgently. No wonder you often feel that the universe conspires against you and that the people around you seek to take what is rightfully yours. The universe is a reflection of what you emanate to it and you know better than anyone how to use words and situations to your advantage – and that is not necessarily a bad thing. However, the ways and means used can be.

Therefore, it is time to look inside and judge yourself and your attitudes with the same critical sense that you use for the outside world. Self-responsibility is necessary for you to realize your personal revolution: achieving all your dreams and goals, and surpassing the expectations that you and the world have placed on your shoulders – and that weight, I know, is big and painful!

By overcoming the challenges that fate has set for you and discovering your true inner self, oblivious to the masks that have been imposed on you throughout your life, you will be able to achieve much more than you imagine. For this, however, it is necessary to put the lies aside and admit your mistakes and limitations. You can try to deceive the whole world, but you can never truly deceive yourself.

EJIONILE'S SHADOW MEDITATION

If the tongue is the soul whip, how do I observe and manage my thoughts and words in order to define what energies I put out to the universe, knowing that all that goes comes back around? What am I communicating, verbally and nonverbally, to the people around me, and am I honestly prepared for the setbacks and other responses of the universe to the vibrations I give out?

17. OSSA

Fire and passion run through your veins

REGENT ORISHAS: Oya, Yemaya and Iyewa

KEYWORDS: Strategic intelligence; generous; tireless worker; great willpower; friendly; charismatic; benevolent; does not hold grudges; clairvoyant and intuitive

The positive influence of Odu Ossa makes you a highly intelligent and active person, capable of accomplishing great deeds in a short period of time. Proactivity and achievement are the keywords of this moment, and if you are not always busy and running against the clock you will not feel complete, will you? Passionate about what you do, you have the gift of moving everything and everyone around you; of making things happen and bringing life and warmth where there was only stagnation.

A tireless worker, you are single-minded, and no effort is too much for you. Your steps are guided by the speed of thunder and the force of storms, and Ossa's fire governs your thoughts and actions. Knowing that success is on the way gives you the courage to face even the greatest challenges, although you urgently need to learn your own limit, body and soul. After all, as much as you want to believe it, you are not a machine.

Benevolent and generous, you do not hesitate to help anyone who asks, assuming for yourself the mission to make up whatever's lacking: money, love, care. In return, you demand that those you've helped are willing to accompany you on your journey at your fast pace – and that won't always be possible. This doesn't mean that you should slow down, nor that people don't love you; you need to recognize that everything and everyone has their own time and rhythm, usually different from yours.

OSSA'S EMPOWERING RITUAL

On a Waxing Moon Wednesday, write your wishes on a piece of white paper, asking Oya for the courage, determination and enthusiasm to pursue your biggest dreams. Cover a pottery plate with cherry, pitanga or strawberry leaves and put the paper on top of them, drizzling it lightly with palm oil. Place a big red apple on the paper, then drizzle it with honey and place nine coins around the apple. Around the plate, place and light nine red or maroon candles. Next day, either eat the apple or bury it in your garden or in a pot plant at your home or workplace.

18. OSSA

When the heart screams, reasoning goes silent

REGENT ORISHAS: Oya, Nanna and Egun (the Ancestors)

KEYWORDS: Overbearing and arrogant; won't listen to anyone and talks too much; is surrounded by false friends; suffers from female harassment and stalking; impulsive; takes all feelings to the extreme; despairs if things are not done their way; tendency to multiple relationships

Odu Ossa's negative regency makes your blood boil at the slightest spark. With no restraint, you say what you think: your tongue is definitely a weapon, and you have a bad habit of not knowing how to use it correctly. You don't listen to anything that is said and still try to mold the truth according to your desires. It doesn't matter if what you believe you've heard has actually been said – you believe it has and now you want war! With that, Odu Ossa's flame burns in your mouth and sets the world on fire, until eventually you realize the fire you've caused and try to put it out – usually too late.

In this moment, feelings are being taken to the ultimate power: when you love, you love violently, surrendering to the point of forgetting yourself and giving your heart and soul to the end. And when that end comes, so much passion automatically turns to hate and indifference, as if an internal off button has been pressed. Such intensity makes you authoritarian and dominating, not accepting anything that happens beyond what you determine and demand. When life shows you that you are not in control of the world, despair and obsession drive you to the brink of madness.

All this intensity being used in the wrong way also finds its end, and when the passion for what you are doing finishes so does the impetus to make the world go round. If at one extreme you accomplish much more and much better than everyone else, at the opposite extreme, stagnation knocks you down like a gale and prevents you from carrying out even the simplest plans. Therefore, your biggest challenge is finding the balance between intensity and inertia. Serenity of actions and thoughts: this is the key to transforming your ways!

OSSA'S SHADOW MEDITATION

When I don't see my wishes, demands and interests attended to in the time and in the way I expect, am I capable of accepting that life has its own time and that winning and losing are part of the process of growing as a person while practicing resilience and resignation? Or do I let anger take over and act in fury to take what's not been given to me? When that's the case, what real and lasting benefit did I ever get from these selfish urges?

19. OFUN

There are times to seed and there are times to flourish

REGENT ORISHAS: Oshalufan (the older Oshala) and Obatala

KEYWORDS: Patient and understanding; consolidates material goods; creates and maintains long-term friendships and relationships; air of authority; generous; great word skill, especially spoken; intelligent; above unkindness; tendency to live many years

Ah, if everyone in the world had your patience and righteousness! Your greatest power is in your voice – that you speak and shut up at the right time and in the exact measure. Likewise, understanding the time and pace of life and agreeing to balance your needs with the needs of others, honoring their experiences and respecting their traumas, seems to be your path to enlightenment.

Under the positive influence of Odu Ofun, your gaze communicates far beyond what words could say and the current moment makes you a great adviser, making people

see you as a natural leader. Past experiences and future directions fit in the palm of your hand and you know the best is yet to come. In fact, this optimism and ability to deal with the most complex situations with the understanding and tranquility of acquired wisdom is one of your greatest qualities right now. If I could give you one single piece of advice, it would be to learn how to apply this serenity from now on, even in face of dangers and despairs yet to come.

By looking into the past and the experiences of those who have gone before, you will be able to understand that constancy and maturity come with experience. From there, while trying to comprehend the steps taken before yours, the answers you are looking for will arrive, and you will finally pace your life's rhythm with the one that resounds all over the universe.

How about taking this time to practice empathy? After all, if you haven't reached enlightenment yet, others around you are far behind, and by humbly leading, listening and advising them, you can learn together to truly experience the peace you so long for amid the chaos of life.

OFUN'S EMPOWERING RITUAL

On a New Moon or Waxing Moon Friday, cook a bowl of white hominy (aka white corn, available from specialist online stores) and drain, reserving the cooking water. Let the hominy and cooking water cool. Put the hominy in a white pottery bowl with a white seven-day candle lit over it, and place your offering as high as possible, praising Orisha Oshala and asking for the serenity to accept things you cannot change, the courage to change what you can, and the wisdom to know how to discern between them. After the candle has burnt, leave the hominy in a river or garden. To use the cooking water, add a gallon (4 liters) of clear water and take it as a bath just before bedtime, putting on white clothes afterward.

20. OFUN

The future will never come while you're attached to the past

REGENT ORISHAS: Oshalufan (the older Oshala) and Obatala

KEYWORDS: Proud, doesn't accept being forced into anything; resistant to renouncing the past; stubborn and unyielding; jealous and possessive; difficulty in finishing what you started; carries the faults of the world in the soul; absorbs anger which then manifests in the body

Odu Ofun's negative regency seems to make time stand still, contrasting with your heart that pulses eagerly for constant news. No matter how hard you try, the impression is that your goals always drag, taking time to be accomplished and, precisely because of that, patience and resignation are not your allies at this time. However, respecting the pace of life is the greatest lesson and nothing good will come from stubbornly trying to accelerate, as you will end up tripping over your own steps.

Everything that comes easy goes easy and it's time to recognize that if life seems to take a long time, it's because the Orishas are preparing lasting successes and achievements for you. What good would it do to fulfill your goals only to see them blow away like dust on the wind because you don't know how to value the effort of the journey? Calm down and be sure that, even if late, fate will not fail you.

You have a strong character and well-based opinions, but inflexibility and excessive pride have often caused you to miss great opportunities by talking too much, forgetting that silence is the way to victory when Odu Ofun is ruling the way. Rather than reacting to the world with stubbornness, wouldn't it be better to balance things out and give in now to conquer the whole in the end?

Still, it won't do any good to cry about what happened, even though you insist on carrying the weight of the world on your back, which slows you down and makes your personal evolution take even longer to happen. It's time to exercise self-forgiveness, lightening the burden of guilt that you carry hidden in your heart.

Your personal revolution starts here. Even if things are not the way you would like them to be, with wisdom and patience they can end according to your wishes. Your attachment to the past and your difficulty finishing the things you start are the main points that prevent the fulfillment of this revolution. Look inside yourself and, even if pride does not allow you to admit your mistakes publicly, seek to correct them internally.

OFUN'S SHADOW MEDITATION

How many weights from past attachments am I carrying through life, feeling the heart heavy and unable to accept the new opportunities destiny has brought; crying and yelling for what has been, but deliberately not recognizing what's yet to come? And how comfortable is it to be in the victim's role, after all?

21. OWARIN

POSITIVE ASPECT

Good luck is only one step ahead

REGENT ORISHAS: Eshu, Oya and Ogun

KEYWORDS: Communicative, makes friends easily; tendency to acquire wealth in youth; ability to start over, like the phoenix; good heart; born entrepreneur; natural beauty and good luck; brave and stubborn, pursues goals

How nice is it to be able to recognize that good luck has always accompanied you even during the biggest storms? With the positive regency of Odu Owarin, self-confidence is your trademark; determination to achieve goals, your life's motto. This regency announces the continuation of winning cycles, giving the strength to conquer prominent positions and even greater goals.

No matter what happens, with your intelligence and creativity you feel like a phoenix rising from the ashes; ever more beautiful, ever stronger. This is how you wake up every day and insist on pursuing your dreams urgently. After all, tomorrow is always uncertain. Living every second to the extreme, at a speed that only you are able to keep up, you don't wait for anything and prefer to pay the price. How about slowing down to enjoy the scenery?

The influence of Orishas Oya and Eshu also bring good luck in business and ease in generating and managing wealth, so it is time to invest in your professional plans and skills. Your know how to delegate tasks, acting with excellence in teams, especially in charge of them. Your dreams and plans are big and point to infinity, but in your eagerness to see them fulfilled you may end up taking on responsibilities that are not yours. Be careful, because when everything is going well you can get the impression there are no dangers. Naivety is your weak point and you risk becoming the victim of freeloaders.

OWARIN'S EMPOWERING RITUAL

On a Waxing or Full Moon Wednesday night, put 11 different crystals (and a personal jewel if you have one) in a glass jar and fill it with water, then cover it to protect it. Light a yellow or orange candle in front of your jar and meditate with it before you, picturing the good luck and wealth you wish in your life. Once the candle has burnt, let the jar rest outside under the dew through the night. Next morning, as soon as you wake up and before speaking to anyone, wash your hands and feet with the jar's water.

22. OWARIN

*When you always say
"Yes" to others, you say
"No" to yourself*

REGENT ORISHAS: Eshu, Oya and Ogun

KEYWORDS: Victim of slander, betrayals, ingratitude and scams; constant nervousness; difficulty saying "No"; risks of spiritual illnesses; lives with persecution and imbalances caused by relationships with two or more others

The negative regency of Odu Owarin announces the dangers of suffering from ingratitude for doing good indiscriminately, making you an easy victim for freeloaders and abusers. It seems that no matter how much you help them, they don't even say "Thank you" – on the contrary, they often go around creating lies and slanders about you, thinking and saying that you did no more than your obligation.

By the way, ingratitude is the biggest problem faced by those like you who haven't learned to say "No". Charity and benevolence are noble sentiments and you practice them with excellence; however, it is necessary to understand that kindness and welfare are different things – while the first is an act from a good heart, the second creates bonds of dependence that can hardly be broken without pain. It's time to remember that not everything you can do for others should be done. This is your life challenge: by learning to say "No" and putting yourself first you will take the first step towards eliminating the pain and guilt that you carry within you.

In addition, you need to accept once and for all that life in society, however communal, must be lived alone, and while under the influence of Odu Owarin this should be taken as a rule. Persecution has been haunting all areas of life: in love, work and personal life there always seems to be a third party who unbalances your choices, making you suffer and lose everything you conquer. So it's time to rethink friendships and business and other partnerships that involve you and two or more other people – unfortunately, you're the one who ends up paying the price for the mistakes of others.

Your sense of urgency in life and in the need to achieve your goals are justified; after all, you've been living with the feeling that your time on earth is coming to an end. To alleviate these anxieties, how about seeking medical and spiritual guidance to achieve the balance between physical, mental and spiritual harmony that you so much desire?

OWARIN'S SHADOW MEDITATION

How many times do I feel like I'm carrying other people's guilt and responsibilities – and usually I am? And how many of those times could I have avoided it by saying out loud that I wouldn't take their weight, instead of keeping silent just to feel that I'm included and accepted?

23. EJILASHEBORA

POSITIVE ASPECT

A cruel truth is better than the sweetest lie

REGENT ORISHAS: Shango

KEYWORDS: Sociable and communicative; polite; skill with the written word; diplomatic and persuasive; intriguing and seductive; ability to perceive nuances

The positive influence of Odu Ejilashebora gives you an aura of royalty and authority wherever you are. Charisma and good mood will guide your steps over the next few weeks, and the time has come to count on other people's help to achieve your biggest goals just for being the way you are – that's what everyone around you has learned to admire and respect.

Intriguing and persuasive, you know the right way to say even the hardest things with a smile on your face. With that in mind, it may be useful to hear what Orisha Shango advises: it is time to get clarity in all kinds of relationships: romantic, familiar or professional. For that to happen, use the sociability and persuasive skills that Odu Ejilashebora gives you for now so that all unresolved issues are finally settled.

At the same time, remember that the balance of justice is impartial, so why not take some time to meditate on your words and actions before pointing fingers? Remember to honor the royalty that Orisha Shango holds with his crown: everyone has the right to be wrong, but no good can come when we lie to ourselves and insist on blaming others without first taking a deep look at our soul and assuming responsibility for our flaws and mistakes. Honesty – with others, of course, but mainly with yourself – is the key that will lead you to success at this point in your life.

Nevertheless, as Ejilashebora is the Odu which celebrates all pleasures of life, its influence brings you a hedonistic breath in the midst of life's urgencies, which you should enjoy so you can remember happiness even when the storms of fate are on you. So take a few days to care for yourself, preparing your favorite food. Or take time during work to grab a coffee with someone you love or the weekend to get outdoors for that break you've been dreaming of. Facing life with seriousness has been your daily routine; enjoy the peaceful moment the gods have given to you.

EJILASHEBORA'S EMPOWERING RITUAL

On a Full Moon Wednesday, write your personal and professional development wishes in pencil on a piece of paper and place it on a plate. Cut a pomegranate horizontally in half and place both halves on the paper with the juicy red seeds face up. On each half, place 6 golden coins and, in between them, a red candle. Surround the offering with 12 pieces of ginger root and 12 corncobs, creating a symbolic sun. While the candle burns, meditate and pray to Orisha Shango to bring you his royalty and wisdom to conquer all challenges and goals in life.

24. EJILASHEBORA

Lying to yourself is the most harmful spell

REGENT ORISHAS: Shango
KEYWORDS: Noisy and explosive; vain; tends towards multiple partners; dreamer, has difficulties in acting; tendency to lies; proud, if contradicted becomes authoritarian and arrogant

The negative influence of Odu Ejilashebora indicates a period when the ego and its whims will speak louder than reason, so it is essential to be aware of your emotions and the way you express them in order to ensure that communication and harmony continue. Therefore, be extra careful with your words and especially with your tone of voice, which may be misunderstood and generate conflict even when you seek peace.

If in its positive aspect Ejilashebora points to the power of charisma, in its negative aspect it is the tyranny of those who try to exercise power out of fear and terror that emerges. In this sense, the time has come to review your attitudes and seek to recognize when and how your vanity and selfishness scream to make you heard. As the saying goes, to be a queen it is not enough to sit on the throne or wear a crown. On the contrary, gold and jewels – whether real or symbolic – will not do any good if no-one sees or hears what you're trying to say. No matter how much you cry, the one who could be royalty becomes a jester, and when that happens, you're the only one to blame for the bad choices taken so far.

The tendency to manipulate reality so that your versions of the facts appear to be true contributes to the distancing of those who once cared about you. In love, business and social life, emotional inconstancy and difficulty in establishing sincere ties are present, and it's necessary to seek a balance between the pleasures of the outside world and the harmony of homelife. No matter how many times a lie is repeated, it will never come true – even if many accept it as the only way to end disputes (and conversations) with you.

In the end, lying to yourself will always be the worst lie … After all, with everything that's happening to you nowadays, who are you trying to fool?

EJILASHEBORAS SHADOW MEDITATION

I claim to be right and fair, praising the gods so that justice is done, but ... looking deeper, am I not actually asking that things turn out the way I want, hiding the fact that I'm not as right as I intend to be and that real fairness would harm me? And how often do I create alternative versions of situations just to feel that I'm righteous, instead of facing the raw truth that says I'm only acting for my own benefit?

25. OJIOLOGBON

POSITIVE ASPECT

Compassion is the path that leads to peaceful living

REGENT ORISHAS: Babaluaiye, Nanna and Egun (the Ancestors)

KEYWORDS: Fair and honest; great inner strength to face difficulties; excellent adviser; docile and kind; good taste, preferring simple things; accumulates knowledge, knowing a little bit of everything; prefers to live in a group than alone

Did you know that you're a source of wisdom and inspiration for others? Under the positive influence of Odu Ojiologbon, the time has come to recognize yourself as such – after all, lack of self-confidence has been one of your weak points. Stop for a moment and notice how they come to you in times of pain and doubt, finding in you a counselor and comforter. You have the power to renew people's hopes so that they trust in the greater good and continue to live – how about taking to yourself the advice you give to others?

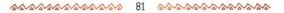

As Odu Ojiologbon represents ends and closures, the symbolic death of what no longer serves us, the influence of Ojiologbon also indicates a period of seclusion and inner observation that, while not bad or foreboding risks, is not suitable for socialising. The routine is becoming more and more tedious and makes you wish to isolate from the world, as if no company is pleasant enough – not even your own. The greater lesson will be found when you understand the difference between solitude and isolation, getting to know yourself by hearing the silent voice of your heart when, finally, you give your mind a rest. Life is not always a party and, at times, finding your own truth in the deepest layers of your own soul can be the key to living in balance amid the chaos of everyday life.

The modern world often requires us to live like superheroes – invincible, infallible and invulnerable to all fate's challenges and issues. For now, however, resignation and contemplation are keywords for the days ahead, teaching that for everything in life there is a time and place: including the times we must surrender to the flow of life and recognize that not everything will always be the way we want – and there is no harm in that.

OJIOLOGBON'S EMPOWERING RITUAL

On a New Moon Saturday, overcook a cup of white cornmeal (white polenta) and let it cool until it's solid. When ready, dissolve the white mass in 3 cups of clear water, add 7 tablespoons of sugar and mix to create a sweet porridge. Before going to sleep, eat a small portion of the preparation and use the rest to prepare a bath to be taken from head to toe, asking Orisha Nana to protect you from health issues and give your mind balance and strength.

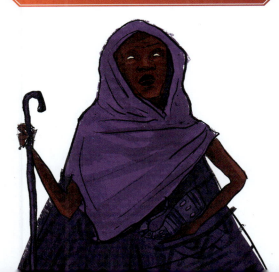

26. OJIOLOGBON

When death calls, there's no place to hide

REGENT ORISHAS: Babaluaiye, Nanna and Iku (the Death)

KEYWORDS: Impressionable and easily influenced; lives in fear of death; strong in public but cries in private; talks too much and doesn't keep secrets; get involved with issues that do not concern you; emotionally dependent

What is the use of seeking answers about which paths to follow if the fear that haunts your soul prevents you from acting and seeking what you want? Under the negative influence of Odu Ojiologbon, the time has come to look inside yourself to seek the light that once shone, but now flickers sadly in the face of the challenges of destiny.

In contrast to the darkness that takes you inside, you have made a tremendous effort to appear strong to the people around you who recognize in you a safe haven to vent their anxieties and doubts. It's as if the universe tried to tell you: "Just like you, others suffer too and that's okay; after all, no pain lasts forever!" However, as a way to avoid taking your own life in hand you give in to other people's issues and, many times, end up blurring the line between advice and intrusion. I know your intentions are always good, but while trying to help others as a way to escape from your own shadows, you've been talking too much and, even without realizing it, revealing secrets and intimacies that were confided in you.

Yes, the world is a dangerous place, but are the threats really so much bigger and stronger than you are able to face? There is a saying that "worse than dying is not feeling alive", and isn't that what you've been doing: accepting your circumstances without even trying to do things differently? The key to this moment in your life is realizing that by letting fate lead the way to avoid having to make decisions for yourself, you are still making the ultimate decision: to leave your life in the hands of the unknown. The question, however, is where will these choices take you, since for those who don't know where they're going, any path will do. Where will you go from here?

OJIOLOGBON'S SHADOW MEDITATION

Even though the world is full of dangers and risks,
how many opportunities in life have I lost by living
scared of the darkness of what could have been,
not realizing there was also light along the way?
And for how long will I keep letting the fear of the
unknown prevent me pursuing and conquering
what I know the Orishas have reserved for me?

27. IKA

"Impossible" is only a matter of opinion

REGENT ORISHAS: Oshumare, Iyewa, Ossain and Iroko
KEYWORDS: Confident and self-assured; ability to create good friendships; predisposition to heroism; courageous, does not hesitate in the face of danger; ease of accumulating wealth and prosperity; material detachment and generosity

Self-confidence is the keyword of the moment under the auspices of Odu Ika in its positive aspect. With that in mind, the time has come to recognize your efforts so far and be proud of everything you have achieved, despite all the challenges of destiny. This is, perhaps, one of the hardest lessons to be learned: to realize and recognize your own worth and celebrate your victories without surrendering to the ego's temptations and letting yourself be dominated by arrogance.

You've been inspiring people around you, often transmitting a certain air of heroism to them – after all, no matter how big fate's challenges are, you face them with your head held high and always find a way to bring out the best in any situation. Even when soul shadows overcome, your posture of self-control and dominion over the world makes others see you as strong and sovereign. How about using this to your advantage and once again moving towards your boldest goals, counting on the good friends you've made along the way?

The only downside is that not everyone around you is willing to continually reinvent themselves like you do. Many look for solidity and stability – which, at this point, you can't offer. The impulsiveness that is natural to your personality can end up creating conflicts with people you care about and even some difficulty in establishing lasting bonds, such as in a love relationship or a career consolidated in a single company. When your biggest pleasure is in the challenge of pursuit, not the conquest of a goal, it can be difficult to attach yourself to what can mean stability and monotony.

Reinventing yourself is an art, but remember that true happiness is only found through balancing what you really are, what you show to the world and what you absorb from everything in that world. In that sense, it might be a good idea to stop for a moment and reflect on what your real goals are and where, exactly, you want to go – maybe you're already there without even noticing.

IKA'S EMPOWERING RITUAL

On a New Moon Tuesday, write your wishes to Odu Ika and Orishas Oshumare and Iyewa on a piece of white paper so they bring you renewal in all areas of life, the capacity to reinvent yourself, the creativity and new ideas for changing all aspects of life that you don't like, and the serenity to understand life's cycles. Place the paper on a banana leaf. Then prepare 2 cups of mashed sweet potatoes and place it over the paper in the shape of a snake, using half a pear as the head and 14 coins as the snake's scales. Decorate the snake's skin with roasted grains of corn, black beans and peanuts; you can also put exotic flowers on the sides of the snake. On the same day, leave your offering by the side of a highroad or at the entrance to a forest.

28. IKA

NEGATIVE ASPECT

To avoid reality only makes you face the same issues again and again

REGENT ORISHAS: Oshumare, Iyewa, Ossain and Iroko

KEYWORDS: Dramatic personality, has a tendency to overexaggerate situations; lives on an emotional rollercoaster; impulsive, takes everything to the extreme; has difficulty trusting others; carries trauma due to physical and sexual violence

As if playing with a powder keg at the edge of a bonfire, the negative influence of Odu Ika in this moment alerts to the dangers of aggression and imminent explosive violence. This is often gratuitous; you've reached your limit and from there all that remains is the leap into the unknown abyss. It's not always easy to see the reality of life and not be hurt when you realize that, despite all your efforts, it seems that happiness is getting farther and farther away. Still, giving in to these impulses will not cause revolution, just more confusion.

Breathe for a moment and, looking inward, seek to recognize how much of all that anguish and hurt comes from the demands you impose on yourself and others. No matter how strong your will, your self-sufficiency and your ability to achieve, not everyone around you is prepared to experience a rollercoaster of emotions like you and demanding it from them will only reinforce the loneliness that adult life has imposed on you. In the same way, just because others can't keep up with your pace it doesn't mean that they don't deserve your trust. As difficult as this may seem, it is possible to delegate tasks and responsibilities to people around you, as long as you can recognize their limitations and, especially, learn who and what to trust.

On the other hand, as an Odu of contrasts and revolutions, Ika often ends up rocking your emotional stability, which can lead you to act aggressively and make decisions based on passion instead of reason. Sometimes yes, sometimes no, always maybe: that way, neither you nor the universe will know which direction to take, so any effort will be in vain. Instead of accelerating and tripping over your own feet while trying to accomplish everything at the same time, how about slowing down and moving forward with the certainty that the path you have taken is the one you really want? Remember: life changes happen one step at a time.

IKA'S SHADOW MEDITATION

Thinking about the smallest goal I wish to achieve, do I honestly know where I am right now, where exactly I want to be and what steps I need to take to get there? And am I prepared and do I have the necessary courage to face the challenges, or do I fantasize that everything around me changes but I don't? If any of my answers about my smallest goal were "No", how do I intend to achieve the biggest one without transforming myself and the way I walk through life first?

29. OBEOGUNDA

POSITIVE ASPECT

*Courage is the fuel that will
take you where you wish to be*

REGENT ORISHAS: Obba, Oya, Yemaya and Ogun
KEYWORDS: Courageous and audacious; always
searching for the new; hard worker; helpful and willing;
carries an eternal desire for conquest

The presence of Odu Obeogunda in your path points
to a period of courage and audacity, during which little
or nothing will be able to prevent you from putting into
practice what you want. The intensity of your feelings and
your sense of confidence make it seem that nothing is as
difficult as people say, giving you the necessary dynamism
to conquer the impossible, transforming the reality around
you according to your wishes, whatever the cost!

All this intensity can seem strange to those who live
in fear of the unforeseen and try to anticipate potential
errors before acting. When asked if you have even
thought about "what ifs", the answer is clear: there is no
"if" when you carry the certainty of success in your soul

and heart. This self-confidence is noticed and admired by the people around you. With this, your voice and your desires will be heard with greater authority, indicating that this is also a favorable period for partnerships and the use of your charisma as a tool of influence – either social, political or romantic.

Although subjective issues can be addressed, in its positive aspect, Odu Obeogunda indicates that it is time to roll up your sleeves and act on practical reality. A provider by nature, work is what gives you reason to live and seems to be your fuel to move forward. This, however, can make you dedicate yourself fully to it, forgetting that money is only good when we can enjoy it. How about directing all this energy to enact plans and dreams that have been postponed, maintaining the balance between search, conquest and delight?

OBEOGUNDA'S EMPOWERING RITUAL

On a New Moon Wednesday, cook 2 cups of corn until it's soft to chew. Let it cool and put it in a pottery bowl, drizzling it with honey and palm oil. On the center of the corn, place a pineapple with a large crown and decorate it with 15 daisies, pink roses or pink/orange geraniums. Write your wishes on 15 paper strips, one wish per piece, and put them between the leaves of the pineapple's crown. Leave your offering on the top of a hill or at the shore, retaining the bowl for future use, and asking Orisha Obba to give you courage and temperance to face life's issues with a good heart and without giving in to the heat of emotion.

30. OBEOGUNDA

NEGATIVE ASPECT

Sometimes the best win is to choose what you're willing to lose

REGENT ORISHAS: Obba, Oya, Yemaya and Ogun
KEYWORDS: Extremist; uncompromising; tendency to experience depression and psychological issues; lonely; undisciplined; jealous; has toxic relationships

Emotional lack of control and extremism mark the days under the negative regency of Odu Obeogunda. Hot or cold, yes or no – it is from opposites that your actions and feelings are made at this moment and any spark is a sign of great danger. Your attitudes and words, even unintentionally, have flirted with violence and the attempt to dominate everyone and everything around you, in any relationship – social, professional or romantic. With so much fire coming out of you, it's natural to feel lonely even in a crowd – after all, who can hold fire in their hands?

You often border on arrogance for believing you can accomplish anything without bearing the natural consequences of your choices. Stubbornness and rebellion guide your steps nowadays, but is everyone really at war against you, as it seems? Seeking balance is the greatest challenge of your destiny, and also your greatest difficulty. After all, for this you must face your greatest fears and accept that your will won't always prevail.

With so much anger inside your heart, sooner or later the body will complain, and this melting pot of emotions will certainly reflect on your psychological aspects: you might feel like you're going crazy; as if any drop could make this overflow and, from there, open the floodgates of your soul like a dam that collapses and destroys everything around.

I know there is no easy way out right now ... So when everything seems to border on despair, the only way is to dive into this feeling until you reach the very bottom of your soul, breathing and recognizing that for everything in life there is a right time – even to stop fighting and allow yourself to heal the wounds the world has caused. The courage to let go of what is bad for us and give up insisting on what is no longer useful is the greatest proof of self-love and self-care that anyone can give themselves. How about starting to do so?

OBEOGUNDA'S SHADOW MEDITATION

Considering this year's most intense life issues and struggles, when I saw myself in affliction and despair, how many of those situations could've been less painful if I'd tried to take a step back and put things in perspective, not letting emotions take control of my decisions? And how many of them could have been avoided if I'd balanced my words and actions, trying to achieve peace instead of simply trying to be right?

31. ALAFIA

POSITIVE ASPECT

No harm can hurt those who live in peace with themselves

REGENT ORISHAS: Orunmila and Eshu
KEYWORDS: Pacifist; curious and searching; volunteer; comprehensive; great humanitarian sense

Have you ever asked yourself what you need to live in peace? Under the positive influence of Odu Alafia, it is time to reflect on your deepest desires and urges, seeking the sincere answer to this question. After all, only by understanding the motivation beneath each of your desires and goals will you be able to understand what's missing so they can be achieved and, finally, celebrated!

Peace is not always the absence of problems. On the contrary: it is through the challenges life imposes on us that we evolve and go beyond limits previously considered insurmountable. Peace also doesn't necessarily mean the abundance of financial resources – after all, what is the use of having it and, due to the hardships of

fate, spending all your fortune on medical treatments or defending yourself against litigation, for example?

At the end of the day, peace is being able to take a deep breath and feel complete; having the inner certainty that you have done your best and, with that, done everything possible up to the present moment. The future? Let it come! After all, you are prepared for it!

Generosity towards and understanding of your fellow humans are your greatest qualities in this moment of life and you will find yourself more empathetic than usual. This can be an excellent opportunity to evolve materially and spiritually, improving your interpersonal skills while using the network of contacts and affections you've been building to achieve your desires and goals through mutual collaboration.

However, be careful not to flirt with the utopian feeling that everything and everyone seeks to do good impartially. By finding the balance between what's real and what's imaginary, reconciling your personal interests and desires with those of the people around you – whether they are dear to you or unknown – you will be able to accomplish great things for yourself and for all those around you, building a legacy that will surely last for generations!

ALAFIA'S EMPOWERING RITUAL

On a Waxing Moon Sunday, cook a bowl of white hominy (white corn) and reserve the cooking water. Let the hominy and cooking water cool. Put the hominy in a white pottery or ceramic bowl. Sew a white flag and write your wishes on it, then paint 16 indigo dots on the flag and place it on top of the hominy. Put your offering in the highest place possible and light a seven-day light-blue candle in front of it, praising all Orishas to protect you and your dear ones, bringing peace and love whatever life's challenges are, and giving you peace of mind and the tranquility to make righteous decisions. To the hominy cooking water, add a gallon (4 liters) of clear water and a pinch of indigo powder and use it as a bath first thing in the morning, without speaking to anyone beforehand. After the candle has burnt, leave the hominy in a river or garden.

32. ALAFIA

A chaotic life is the result of chaotic choices

REGENT ORISHAS: Orunmila and Eshu
KEYWORDS: Fanciful and utopian; indecisive; lives in affliction; fears losing everything and everyone

The negative influence of Odu Alafia brings constant affliction in face of the apparent chaos of the outside world, which is reflected inwardly and, even in the simplest situations, brings difficulty in making choices and decisions. The universe is open in front of you, full of possibilities and alternatives and, precisely for this reason, deciding to follow a single path by giving up other options tortures your soul.

The constant fear of hurting and losing people, opportunities and yourself ends up causing stagnation, preventing you from leaving the dream world and acting to get your plans and goals off the page. I know … In today's world, where it seems that everyone thinks solely and exclusively about themselves, it becomes difficult to balance your personal desires with those of people around you in an attempt to respect and value their ambitions and dreams. Even though a key aspect in building your self-esteem is realizing that, despite everything, your opinions and desires are also important and can always be valued and sought without prejudicing the people you love and care for.

Still, it can be difficult to rationalize feelings when you seem to live in the eye of the hurricane. Whether at work, in friendships or in love relationships, it's time to strengthen existing bonds and establish new bonds of trust and loyalty that will soothe your heart. People come and go in our lives; nothing in the world is permanent or immutable. However, living in fear only causes anguish. Just be careful, for choosing to view the world from a positive place, you often also choose to ignore the malice of the world. This ends up hurting and frustrating you when you're forced to face situations where others' motivations aren't as sweet as you thought.

With that in mind, what about trying to calm your mind and allow yourself to hear the voice of creativity that is unique to you? I'm sure you will be able to find ways to reconcile your desires with those of others and still favor situations in which everyone wins. At the very least, seeking this way of valuing yourself and others is the most commendable way to avoid assuming sole responsibility for solving all the conflicts in the world. After all, no-one said you're the redemptive hero of the universe … did they?

ALAFIA'S SHADOW MEDITATION

When I look sincerely at my life deceptions and delusions, how many times could I have protected my heart and feelings by admitting to myself that life is a lonely road instead of an "all for one and one for all" fantasy? And what will it take from now on so I can stop trying to please everyone around me and put my own interests first?

33. WAXING MOON

May there be light over darkness ...
It's time to rise and shine!

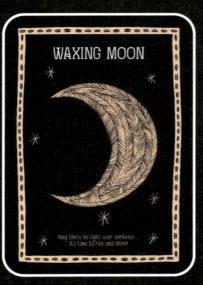

This is the phase when the moon comes out of the darkness and begins to be reborn, lighting up the sky. Therefore, it is a time to start new projects, get new ideas and plans into action and allow yourself to stop and smell the roses. For the next days, the growing energy of Waxing Moon will conduct the situations of your life, so you'd better be ready to make the most out of all the chances destiny presents you.

Creativity and the capability to find resources and alternatives where there are only shadows and doubts will mark this moment in life. Therefore, if the Odus revealed in your cards present their negative aspect, try to see between the darkness they bring and let your inner voice guide you to the light that will overcome all anguish in the near future, just as a river gently flows to the ocean.

On the other hand, if the cards present the positive aspect of Odus, rise and shine: it's time to accept all the gifts and blessings the gods are bringing to your life, allowing them to seed and root their energy so you can flourish and grow, becoming the best version of yourself.

34. FULL MOON

*Fully living the powers
of the universe*

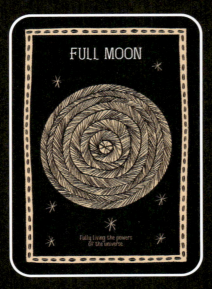

FULL MOON

Fully living the powers
of the universe

This is the phase when the moon is most visible and bright, reigning fully in the sky. It is during this period that the spiritual energies reach their peak and consolidate, vibrating strongly and, therefore, strengthening the achievement and fulfillment of your goals.

At the same time, it is also the phase when things can get a little bit out of control, as its energy has grown and expanded and it's now reaching the most intense and powerful time. With this in mind, if a negative Odu presents during your consultation, it's time to take a step back, try to put things in perspective and don't despair: just like the moon, every situation in life has its phases and things will change soon. Of course, for it to be good for you, it's fundamental that you understand your responsibility over all that is happening to you right now.

On the other hand, if a positive Odu card presents itself, embrace its blessings and remember to be thankful for all you have right now. The Full Moon energy indicates that situations will intensify until they harmonize and consolidate, allowing you to enjoy them while getting prepared for the new things that surely will come your way.

35. WANING MOON

It's time to banish all evil

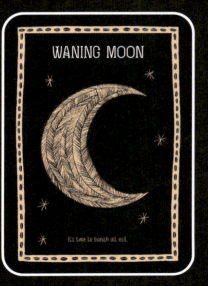

This is the phase in which the moon decreases in brightness until disappearing and dying for a few days. It is a time of symbolic death and resurrection, making it the right time for the closure of everything that is no longer needed or desired, the banishment of negative energies, the release and ending of situations, and the reversal of unwanted situations. With that, it's time to reflect on what you want – after all, not everything we want is good for us.

When a negative Odu card presents itself with the Waning Moon, it's time to retreat and admit that you can't have it all, no matter how hard you try. Considered a negative phase of the moon, this card reinforces the negative aspect of the Odu and usually indicates that there's no escape from the Odu's unfortunate predictions. At the same time, because it's also considered a banishment moon phase, one can seek to cut off the Odu's negative influence with magic rituals.

On the other hand, if the Waning Moon shows up with a positive Odu, it's time to protect yourself from the outside world, avoiding envy by keeping your victories quiet for a while. It can also mean that your achievements have reached their full potential for now, so it's time to calm down, count your blessings and enjoy what you have instead of pursuing more and more, as it could make all that is already there go away.

36. NEW MOON

Looking within can reveal the mysteries of the universe

NEW MOON

Looking within can reveal the
mysteries of the universe.

This is the phase when the moon is not visible in the sky. It's preparing to be reborn in its new cycle. Therefore, it is a period of energetic instability, full of mysteries and insecurities, indicating a moment more favorable to reflection than to action. The oldest traditions of magic teach us that in order to be (re)born, one must first withdraw and symbolically die – this is the New Moon.

Therefore, if a negative Odu card presents itself with New Moon, it's time to look deeper into your soul, investigating what happened in the near past so you're facing these issues right now. Only this way will you be able to reveal the secret possibilities that the New Moon keeps under its shadows and, in the near future, shine brightly when the Waxing Moon rises.

On the other hand, if a positive Odu card shows up, it's time to meditate on how to keep what you have already achieved and, slowly and carefully, allow it to flourish in the near future. Introspection and meditation on what was, what is and what will be are the keys to re-create happiness and success in your life.

Also, the New Moon indicates the numbness of things, so it's a time when things probably won't change – for better or for worse. Just as during war there's a time to attack, there's also time to heal your wounds, and this time is now!

ABOUT THE AUTHOR

A Gaucho (southern-born Brazilian) based in São Paulo, Diego de Oxóssi graduated in Management Processes from Anhembi Morumbi University and Integral Systemic Coaching from FEBRACIS Institute. He is Priest of Kimbanda and Babalosha of Candomblé, working with personal development, consulting and spiritual guidance throughout Brazil and abroad.

For more than 20 years, Diego de Oxóssi has been dedicated to researching and presenting courses, lectures and workshops on Afro-Brazilian religions, their regional forms of expression and the integration of their rituals into society.

Responsible for Editora Arole Cultural – a Brazilian publishing company specialising in mind, body and spirit publications about African-origin spirituality, in 2015 he released his first book, *Desvendando Exu* (published in English as *Traditional Brazilian Black Magic*), in which he demystifies the controversial character of African-based religions and shows that, despite the erroneous conflation with the Devil, Eshu is the biggest friend, defender, and companion of the faithful.

Between 2016 and 2018, Diego de Oxóssi wrote and published *As Folhas Sagradas* – a bestselling series in Brazil that was published in the USA in 2022, entitled *Sacred Leaves: A Magical Guide to Orisha Herbal Witchcraft*.

In 2019, Diego received the Young Talent of the Editorial Market award by *PublishNews*, the biggest Brazilian online publishing trade magazine, and has participated in international book fairs including London, Bologna, Buenos Aires and Frankfurt.

In 2020, Diego released *Odus de Nascimento* (the English edition, *African Numerology*, was published in 2022), teaching the secrets and mysteries of African numerology by the interpretation of Odus archetypes, while taking the reader in an inner journey of soul growth and awareness. This oracle was inspired by the success of *Odus de Nascimento*.

www.diegodeoxossi.com.br
@diegodeoxossi
/diego.oxossi

ABOUT THE ILLUSTRATOR

Breno Loeser is an illustrator, artist, and designer with a masters degree in Science of Religions from UFS – Ceará's Federal University. He works in financial technology in addition to freelancing in branding, editorial, and art. He also coordinates his own online store, brenoloeser.com, with signed pieces and fine art reproductions. He is initiated to Orisha Logunedé and a lover of the finer things in life. In 2021, Breno became the illustrator responsible for the *Orishas for Children* collection, published in Brazil by Arole Cultural, the mind body spirit publishing house headed by Diego de Oxóssi.

www.brenoloeser.com
@brenoloeser
/loeser.breno

⚬◉ ACKNOWLEDGEMENTS ◉⚬

A *frican Gods Oracle* is to dedicated to my mother Marines and my sister Camila. To my grandmother Nelza, her sister Aura, and to my godmother Mara, who first introduced me to spirituality and to the mysteries of fortunetelling.

To Priestess Ieda de Ogun, for all the affection and companionship in these more than 12 years. To the warrior Anderson de Ogun, who supports me in every battle of life and believes in the mission that the Orishas assigned us. And to dear Aluísio, who trusts me with his secrets and keeps mine as his own.

To Eshu 7 Facadas, my friend, my drunken rascal and my eternal guardian, for opening all crossroads of the world so my word can reach everywhere. To Oshossi (in Portuguese, Oxóssi, whose name I carry), the hunter of a single arrow, master of the jungle and of my life, for everything I have accomplished so far.

And to everyone who encouraged or doubted me: both are my daily fuel!